What-a-Mess the Good

Frank Muir
Illustrated by Joseph Wright

First published 1978 by Ernest Benn Limited.
25 New Street Square, London EC4A 3JA
and Sovereign Way, Tonbridge, Kent TN9 1RW.

© Frank Muir 1978.
Illustrations © Joseph Wright 1978.
Printed in England by W.S. Cowell Ltd, Ipswich.
ISBN 0 510-12400-3

Ernest Benn
London & Tonbridge

At five minutes past four on a sunny Sunday in late July,
What-a-mess had a brilliant idea. He was lying idly
in the long grass, trying to think of something interesting to think
about and playing with a basket of knitting wool,
when suddenly the brilliant idea popped into his head and stayed there.

It was only the fourth idea he had ever had in his life,
because besides being fat, small and exceedingly scruffy,
he was also a very young puppy;
but he knew instantly that the idea was a brilliant one.

And like all brilliant ideas it was very simple.
He would turn over a new leaf. From this very second on
he would become a Good Dog. And then perhaps he would grow up
like his mother, whom he loved, who was not only good,
but was also tall and beautiful.
The more he thought about it the more he liked it.

"I will be more than Good," he said to himself, "I will be the Goodest!" (He wasn't very good at grammar, either.)
It was all so exciting that he pointed his nose up to the sky and did his baying-at-the moon noise. Then he grabbed the wool-basket with his teeth and hurled it high in the air. The balls of wool flew out, transforming the old, dead plum tree into a rose bush.

"I will be kind and considerate and people will stop saying 'What-a-mess!' and will call me by my real name. They will thank me for my good deeds and pat me, saying 'Well done, Prince Amir of Kinjan'. Or even better, I will be voted World Champion Best-Behaved Dog (Small, Fat, Afghan Puppy Class) at Crufts. And they will name a dog-food after me and put my face on television!"

He jumped up, hurtled at full speed down the drive and did
his new trick of locking his legs at the last moment,
skidding to a halt with his nose an inch away from the gate.
A great shower of gravel flew through the air, filling
a passing lady's shopping bag.

"Oh, how good it feels to feel good!" cried What-a-mess.
"Now – to do my good deed!"

He paused, thinking hard. Then – "Got it! Ants!"
Ever since the hot weather had set in, the lady of the house had been saying, "Look! Ants everywhere. I wish someone would *do* something about them!"

So, he would rid the household of ants. The family had gone out for a picnic, taking his mother with them as a treat, and he had the whole place to himself. What a nice surprise they would have when they got back to find that some good puppy had exterminated every ant in the house and garden. Perhaps, if he had enough time, every ant in the world. That would be a good deed indeed.

The first ant he found was in the huge pile of logs neatly stacked against the wall next to the greenhouse.

What-a-mess had to creep up on the ant so that it wouldn't escape, which meant climbing up the logs to the top of the stack. "Farewell!" he barked. The deed was done with a swift swipe of a paw.

It was all rather exciting; the thrill of the hunt, the feeling of doing good, and the musical tinkle of breaking glass as the log-pile began to capsize and the logs tumbled down onto the greenhouse.

The second ant was easy. As What-a-mess loped round the corner of the garden shed, he saw the ant making its way slowly across the front tyre of a bicycle. This was propped against the side of the shed ready to ride to the station in the morning.

Without a moment's hesitation, What-a-mess leaped forward and bit. The ant stood no chance. The puppy had a little trouble getting his tooth out of the tyre, but when he finally managed it he was rewarded by a hissing noise and a stream of cool air playing pleasantly over his face.

Ant number three was much more difficult. Ant-hunting may look easy, but on a hot afternoon the walking about is tiring. At one stage he almost gave up. He was trotting about the lawn in an ant-hunting position, eyes down, not looking where he was going, crouching low, when he rammed his head into a croquet hoop.

But, good puppy that he was, he would not give up.
He was determined to rid the world — and the household —
of three ants. He had decided to limit his campaign to three ants,
partly because it was much more difficult than he thought,
but mainly because he could only count up to three.
(He knew lots of other numbers like a hundred, and sixty-two,
and eight, but he wasn't sure where they came.)

He found his third and final ant in the house.
He saw it first in the drawing-room, running along a bookshelf.
In a flash, he pulled all the books onto the carpet;
but the ant had disappeared. With a patience unusual in a puppy
so young, he picked up each book in his teeth and
tried to shake the ant out. The ant had vanished.

Where was it? Not in the bedrooms. He pulled all the sheets and blankets off the beds and rolled on them.
He even got his teeth into the clothes hanging in the wardrobes and ripped them off their hangers. But no ant emerged.

Bathroom? All clean and shiny. A wandering ant could be spotted in a second. But no ant wandered.
Behind the glossy, plastic wallpaper? He found that if he worried a bit of wallpaper with his claws, he could lift off enough to get a grip with his teeth. He could then rip it off the wall in great sheets. It was only when he was up to his neck in strips of wallpaper that he had to admit that the ant was not there.

Then he pottered into the kitchen to find something to eat; a lick of butter from the dish or a tongueful of sugar from the bowl. And he saw the ant. There it was, in the middle of the kitchen floor, busily trying to carry off a crumb of bread about forty times its own size.

Leaping silently onto the top of the refrigerator —
all Afghans can jump like cats — What-a-mess went straight
into the attack. He reached into a cupboard with his paw
and pushed a large bag of flour in the direction of the ant.
But he did not push hard enough. The bag dropped
straight down onto the cooker, burst with a dull "plop"
and everything went white for a moment.

The next item in the cupboard was a heavy bottle. What-a-mess got a paw behind it and pushed with all his might. The bottle shot across the kitchen. It hit the opposite wall and began to make lolloping sounds as a stream of cooking oil spread slowly across the kitchen floor.

The ant by this time had worked his crumb of bread across to the opposite side of the kitchen. Above it, What-a-mess saw that there was a shelf of large, brightly-coloured tins. Just then, he heard the sound of a car coming up the gravel drive. He knew that he would have to work fast if he was to finish his good deed before the family came in. Using both paws, he pushed all the tins off the shelf.

The first one missed and hit the mixing machine, covering it with bright yellow paint. The second and third also missed and spread blue and green paint across the walls and floor. But the third tin was right on target. As it flew through the air, half a gallon of thick, bright scarlet paint burst from the tin. It engulfed the ant and his bread in a huge, red lake. "I've done it!" barked What-a-mess, his tail wagging happily.

And then the family walked in.

The next hour was the worst he had ever experienced in his short, fat life. The family kept running up and down the stairs and shouting, which frightened him.
The lady cried a great deal, and as the man went from room to room his shouting got louder. Then he tried to go to a neighbour for help; but something was wrong with his bicycle. Suddenly he saw the greenhouse and he sat down and began to cry too. The lady gave him a large glassful of medicine from a bottle.

What-a-mess's mother hurried the terrified puppy out of the house and told him not to come back until everybody had gone to bed.

It was very late when he squeezed himself through the cat-door. This was more difficult than usual because the paint which had splashed onto his coat had picked up a thick covering of leaves and twigs and then dried hard.

"What a mess!" cried his mother when she saw him.

"Why are they so angry with me?" whimpered What-a-mess, as he settled into his basket. "I was trying to be *good*! The lady didn't like ants so I got rid of them for her. Not one ant but *three* ants! I was only trying to help!"

"You just don't *think*," said his mother. "You get an idea in your head and away you go without thinking of the consequences. Think first before acting. Do you understand?"

"Yes," What-a-mess whispered, settling himself down to sleep.
He had forgotten how hungry he was.
His small, but in its way large, tummy was rumbling from lack of food.
What had his mother said? "Think before acting!"

"I *think*," he whispered to himself, "I *think* — I will eat a bit of my basket." He bit into it. It was delicious, crisp and biscuity.

So he ate two inches of his basket evenly all round, crunching it up well.
And in two minutes, feeling much, much, much better,
he drifted off happily into a deep, untroubled puppy sleep.